Orri and Orca

Written by Ida Surjani

Illustrated by Ida Surjani & J.A. Gunnarsson

Copyright © 2014 by Ida Surjani

All rights reserved.
No part of this book may be reproduced or transmitted in any form or by any means without express written permission from the author, except in the case of brief quotations embodied in critical articles and reviews.
Please refer all pertinent questions to the publisher.

ISBN 978-9935-9204-0-9

Ida Surjani, Kópavogur - Iceland

www.idasurjani.com

DEDICATION

I dedicate this book to my lovely son, J.A. Gunnarsson who will be celebrating his 10th birthday this year.

ACKNOWLEDGEMENTS

A special thanks:

To my wonderful friend as well as my former professor, Dr. Suchitra Mouly, for her excellent suggestions and tips as well as editing the book.

To my son, J.A. Gunnarsson for doing some drawings for the book.

To my husband Gunnar for helping me out with the computer issues.

This is a story of a little boy who lives in Iceland. His name is Orri. Orri is 8 years old. He does not like dogs or cats or fish or other pets. He is actually terribly afraid of dogs, cats and other animals.

On a school trip, Orri saw a large poster with many whales from a nearby library. He became fascinated with those whales, particularly orca or killer whale. It is a type of whale that has black colour on top and white colour on its underside.

Orri loved orcas so much. He always wanted to see orcas. He also hoped to have an orca in his home!

Orri was extremely excited as he said to his father, "Dad, can we have an orca in our home? How about we catch an orca?"

Orri's father replied, "Hm….I think it's impossible, son. Do you know how big an orca is? And where and how're you gonna keep it?"

Orri replied, "I have thought about it all, dad. We will build a giant aquarium and have an orca in it," whispered Orri to his father excitedly. "We can place the aquarium in the living room" continued Orri with a twinkle in his hazel eye. "What do you think, dad? Don't you think we can do it together?" And then Orri convinced his father by saying, "I promise I will help you build it dad. Can we make that happen?"

Orri's dad answered that it is impossible to make a big aquarium and have an orca in it. But he promised that they could go to see orcas. "We can go on a boat tour and see whales. And if we are lucky enough we may be able to see orcas as well. What do you think? Do you like to go on a boat? Aren't you afraid of being on a boat?" asked Orri's dad as his heart went out for his son's longing for an orca in his own house.

On one weekend, Orri with his mom and dad drove to Grundarfjördur. It is a town in the north of the Snæfellsnes peninsula in the west of Iceland. It is a small but very beautiful town. They went for a whale watching tour from there.

It took about two to three hours to Grundarfjördur from Orri's place in Kópavogur.

The journey itself was not easy as Orri became easily bored. He kept asking, "are we near the place, dad?" And also, "how long is the journey?" Orri was impatient. He could not wait to see orcas.

After two and a half hours of driving they finally arrived at the venue for a whale watching tour. There were about twenty other people, mostly foreign tourists who loved to see whales in their natural habitat.

It was a windy, cold and rather cloudy day in late March 2013. The boat kept sailing for almost one and a half hours and there was nothing to see except the vast expanse of the ocean and birds flying around in the sky. But then suddenly the tour guide shouted, "Twelve o'clock!" It meant that one could see something at twelve o'clock position or straight ahead position.

3 dolphins jumped out of the water at 12 o'clock position

Orri and his parents and also people on the boat were very excited and observed carefully to the area being told for some sightings of either whales or dolphins.

Wow, it was an incredible sight! There were a whole pod of dolphins swimming and jumping around and they were so very close to the boat. They moved very freely and oh so quickly!

Orri was very excited and happy as he shouted "Dad, look at those baby orcas. Oh look here's another one. Another baby orca! And oh those are another ones as well! You see? One, two, three and that's also four, five and do you see them? Oh there're some others! They jump!"

Orri kept counting and pointing while also watching some dolphins. He thought those dolphins were orca's babies.

Then the boot turned around as it was time to go back to the original marina and Orri occasionally saw few dolphins on the way back. As Orri realised that the tour was almost over and they were heading back, he disappointedly said, "Why did I see only baby orcas? Where are their mothers and fathers?" he asked his parents.

Orri's parents tried to pacify Orri by saying that those dolphins were as cute as orcas. But Orri was not pleased. "These are little orcas, they are just babies. I want to see the big ones, dad. I want to see their moms and dads!"

Orri tried to call out for orcas a few times, "Orcas...orcas…where are you...where are you? Orcas...come out and play. I am Orri, your friend."

However, no orcas were to be seen. They did not see any orcas on that boat trip and Orri was disappointed as only an eight year old could be.

Two months after the boat trip, Orri and his parents were travelling again. This time the trip was to the north of Iceland. They were on a whale watching tour again. The boat started in a lovely town named Husavík. Orri was again hoping to see orcas in this area.

The boat was soon sailing. The sun was shining but the weather was still cold, but importantly there was not much wind. They had a good start for a successful boat tour that day.

Husavík Harbour, North Iceland

Orri was quiet with his own thoughts and hopes of seeing his beloved orcas. It was about thirty minutes or so and the tour guide suddenly announced to the people on the boat with his codes: "three o'clock," and then "nine o'clock," and continued "six o'clock" for directions of the possible sightings.

Orri and his parents, along with the other people on the boat were soon totally absorbed in watching whales and dolphins from the left, then moved to the right and then at the back and also at the front side on the boat. They all kept moving to get as many sightings as they could.

Suddenly, out came a gigantic whale blowing and jumping out of the sea and it was so very close to the boat. Orri was so taken aback at this unexpected sighting that he shouted "I saw it! It's a humpback whale, I know it! I saw it!" And then "oh it's so terribly big!"

Humpback Whale

Orri also saw some fin whales as he shouted, "Over there, look, that's a fin whale!" Those whales kept coming in and out of their view, moving with amazing speed given their size. Orri was excited to see so many whales.

Then it was time for the boat to turn around. Orri said, "Hmm…I still have not seen any big orcas, dad…where are they?" He kept repeating, "where are they, dad?"

Orri's parents explained that it was quite possible that some orcas have travelled somewhere else to another part of the world. Those orcas would usually leave before summer and would be coming back later to Iceland in winter time.

Orri did not understand the explanation, and he seemed to be disappointed as he said, "Possibly they do not exist anymore, dad? Do they?" He continued "Do big orcas really exist in here? I think there are no orcas in here, dad. Perhaps they are somewhere else, but not in here. They are possibly overseas right now. They are obviously not in here! What do you think, dad?"

Orri's dad answered, "Hmm….I think it's quite possible, son. We are probably too late. Those orcas might have travelled else where.
But don't worry, someday we'll see orcas, big ones, son" assured Orri's dad to his disappointed and rather dejected son.

After that boat trip, Orri's parents wondered what they could do to help Orri overcome his disappointment. Would he naturally outgrow it? Orri's dad was planning to go for another boat trip as orcas usually would come back to Iceland in winter. But Orri's mom said that Orri would be totally devastated if they were not lucky and could not see any orcas. They were afraid of giving false hopes to Orri and make things worse for him.

Time passed so quickly and it was almost a year when Orri and his parents went to the first boat tour in Grundarfjördur. They were in the same town again. But this time they were not on a boat tour. They were coming to a birthday party of a distant cousin who lived in a farm outside Grundarfjördur.

Before going to the party they stopped by in a gas station not too far from the marina. Orri was looking far away at the sea and he felt he saw something there. His gaze kept going back to one specific spot again and again. He suddenly told his parents that he saw something black and big jumping out of the water as he shouted excitedly, "I just saw an orca! I am sure it's an orca!"

Orri and his parents walked closer to the marina so that they could see much better. As they came closer they saw there were a group of five orcas swimming not too far from the marina. Orri's face registered a gamut of feelings: excitement, happiness, shock and thrill as he said, "Those are the real orcas, the killer whales that I have been searching for. Those are the real ones. Ohh …I am so glad. I finally see big orcas, very big, and so many of them!"

Those orcas were chasing each other. They jumped out of the water and landed on their back and sometimes also on their side. They also released water through their blowholes.

"Are those orcas playing with each other, dad? They look they're having much fun," asked Orri to his father. "Yes, son, they're just like us. Orcas play with their friends or family members. They're not alone."

Orri replied to his father. "Yes, they do enjoy playing with each other, dad."

Orri watched the ocean with his orcas in them for a long time with total absorption and he finally said, "Orca is so cute. But it is also so terribly big. We really have no place for him at home." As Orri continued saying to his dad, "If we take just one orca to our home, he will get lonely without his family and friends and it's not good to be alone, dad."

Then Orri continued watching those orcas for few minutes until they were finally swam further and further away.

"Orcas are my friends, I love you orcas!" Said Orri while he waved his hand and cheerfully said, "bye-bye orcas, see you later!" Orri's face was happy and serene as he knew that his orcas were happy with their friends in the ocean and that the ocean was their home.

THE END

ABOUT THE AUTHOR

Ida Surjani is a stay at home mom who lives in Kópavogur, Iceland. She loves travelling, painting as well as cooking.

Orri and Orca is Ida's first children's book and this book is the first series of her children's book called "Orri." This book is inspired by a real life incident with her son, a lovely boy who has an autism spectrum disorder. The little boy's incredible love for orcas and his desire to see as well as to own an orca and some memorable events that follow become the basis for this story. The boy's simple conversations to his dad are strongly emphasised in this book to keep young children as well as adults engaged to the scenes while reading this book.

The opportunity to have lived and studied in 3 different countries equipped the author to write this story in three different languages: English, Icelandic and Indonesian. She hopes that this story may touch the hearts of both children and adults.

www.ingramcontent.com/pod-product-compliance
Lightning Source LLC
Chambersburg PA
CBHW041538040426
42446CB00002B/143